Song of the Overcast
Poems

by

Beverly Voigt

Finishing Line Press
Georgetown, Kentucky

Song of the Overcast
Poems

Copyright © 2022 by Beverly Voigt
ISBN 978-1-64662-768-4 First Edition
All rights reserved under International and Pan-American Copyright Conventions. No part of this book may be reproduced in any manner whatsoever without written permission from the publisher, except in the case of brief quotations embodied in critical articles and reviews.

ACKNOWLEDGMENTS

"In Advent" appears in *Sonora Review*, Issue 77.

Many thanks to:
My writing groups, for their thoughtful critiques
The broader writing community, for their constant search for the art in themselves and in others
Carine Topal, for her generous mentorship and friendship
My friends, for support, therapy, and many adventures
My family, for their unwavering love

Publisher: Leah Huete de Maines
Editor: Christen Kincaid
Cover Art: Beverly Voigt
Author Photo: Stanley Okimoto
Cover Design: Elizabeth Maines McCleavy

Order online: www.finishinglinepress.com
also available on amazon.com

Author inquiries and mail orders:
Finishing Line Press
PO Box 1626
Georgetown, Kentucky 40324
USA

Table of Contents

Second Blossoming 1

The Unfinished Nest 2

Vigil, Late September 3

Moon Jelly 4

The Host and the Holder 5

Pontoon 7

The Draw 8

To a Young Cottonwood 9

For the Attenuated 11

Each Spring, These Words 12

Brother 14

Among the Ruins 16

Summer Nights, I Fall Asleep on the Back Porch 18

That Autumn in Pennsylvania 19

To the Animal 20

Between Waves 22

Grief Is Thorns on the Orange Tree 24

Bread = Snow 25

Openings 26

Dead as I Am 28

Overcast 30

In Advent 31

For Doug (1957–2018)
In Memoriam

Second Blossoming

> *"There is only one question:*
> *how to love this world"*
>   —Mary Oliver, from "Spring"

One young spring, when the crabapple tree
bloomed, I so loved the pink-white flowers—

forgetting the hard, sour fruit that would come
later in the year—that I gathered the fallen

and placed them around the yard as though
they had sprouted there, a second life

in the sun. My mother yelled from the porch:
Pick them up before your father gets home. It looks

like dirty tissues blew all over the yard. In time
I forgave her for this, as she forgave me

for so many transgressions. Not with words
but with a new attention, a quiet grace

toward one another. Years later, when I am home
for a visit, she says, *I have something to show you.*

A package of paper napkins, pink and gold,
she had found at the drugstore. A print

of peonies. Here was her love for the trifling,
for the humble discovery. Here was her love

for the beauty in the world, for hope,
and in what small packages it may be found.

The Unfinished Nest

We were like the cobbler's children
with no shoes—the builder's home

was only half-built. Exposed plumbing, rafters,
electrical wires. Ceilings and walls open

to the dark spaces. Pink insulation in rolls
on the floor like raveled hay. For years

we hung Easter eggs and Christmas ornaments
from nails in studs. Draped tinsel over bare

beams. It was like living on the underside
of embroidery—the stitches, the seams that held us

together, visible. We could step through that latticework
as though entering a dream—new doorways into old

spaces, the steps behind the steps, the other sides
of walls. A started-and-stopped world. Half-made rooms

full of cribs and makeshift beds—as though we were birds,
our nest a collection of found objects—twigs,

lint. Bits of paper. Metal. Like the bower-bird's
bower, the weaver's woven home. Nest of frail

hopes. And we were a clutch of nine small worlds,
sky-blue, dappled little things with feathers.

Vigil, Late September

I came to the meadow to look for my brother
though I knew he was home, where his death

lay biding. I looked for him among the goldenrod,
for answers in their overpowering number.

I looked for him in the surrounding woods, among
flickering beech and oak. In abandoned nests

of thatch. But he was not to be found with the still-green
and the goldening, or in the mist riding low

along the creek. When I saw the house I thought
shelter, but it stood as skeletal as my brother's

backbone. Built of tree limbs and lichen, it framed
the preparatory forest. Were the goldenrod

bright lamps in its windows? Or smoldering gods
in that wide plain of autumnal light?

Moon Jelly
    (Aurelia labiata)

It blooms in the dark
    waxes pale

translucent

as the moon
    at daybreak, pink

glow of its craters

It is the moon's
    dream of itself

in a nightdress

pulsing, swooning
    among the rippling stars

The Host and the Holder

The church calls it a pyx—to me it looks like a drugstore pillbox.
Round, bright gold. A creaky opening, meager clasp. Two concentric

whorls of silver etched into the top. It held the wafers my mother
delivered to the homebound on Sunday mornings, my father waiting

in the car. He has given it to me now, years after her death. But
my secular heart feels unworthy. I honor some traditions: the prayer

to Saint Anthony for something lost, the red candle I light
in her memory. I love the church but mostly for its echoes. My family

filling a long pew. The slow pool of voices. The prayers
for everything—after loss, for a happy death, for the morning

and for the evening. The Mysteries: joyful, luminous, sorrowful,
glorious. The dark songs of Advent, in minor chords. The reverberating

alleluias. The word *alleluia*. And the poetry: *Like a deer that longs
for running streams, my soul longs for you.* And I love the church

for its echoes of the natural world: the vaulted light, the windows—
great shattered sheets the sun pours its light through, sending color
      down

like pools of bright fallen petals. The story of Jesus, born into hay
like a bird. How the rituals draw me when I need a home. How

they satisfy my hungry heart. I can't separate them from memories
of my mother: how good she was. How quietly good. I believed

in her body, her warmth. Her large laugh, small shoulders. Soft
hands. Until I saw her body in the bed I didn't believe in the soul,

hers was so clearly gone. Mouth open, empty. Something
tarry left on the pillow. I think of how she performed her duty,

lighting the candle, intoning the words, placing the host
into the grateful mouth of the confined. And I hold this holder

until it lends its metallic scent. Until it warms in my cupped,
worshipful hands.

Pontoon

When my father retired
      he came alive.
On his new boat
      he sets forth
on the green
      Monongahela
like Lewis and Clark
      before him.
A few miles
      downstream
he makes a slow
      wide turn
and comes back
      but when he learns
to navigate the locks
      he'll sail
past the rusted mills
      and harshness
of his youth
      to the Ohio
then follow the water
      south to the gulf
and the great
      wide sea.

The Draw

There and gone in the slow air
        a narrow rope of light
across my doorway

I've seen him that made it, quiet
        by the tree
near the center of the wheel
        with a strength that pulls
the nearest branch
        closer

The moth has been a week
        in the house
clinging to the screen
        holding no memory
one moment
        to the next
only its draw
        toward the light

I dread its leaving
        once it flies into fear
and loses all those days
        of desire

To a Young Cottonwood

A smell of dust. Of drying earth, of grasses
beginning to lie down.

I find a possum, huddled to the earth, unmoving—
freshly killed, I think, but with no marks,

fur intact. Turning it over with my foot
I am surprised at its lightness—and find only

bones beneath, an undisturbed skeleton.
Yellowish ivory of the spine, long incisors—

picked clean from below, the fur simply a blanket
tucked in over the bones. Ghost-blown. I remember

you, young cottonwood, when you were planted.
About my height, spindly, propped. That was before

I knew your name, learned your ways. Before I realized
I am weightless in this world, craving gravity.

I've known you many summers and falls, watched
you change, your arms shade bush-sunflowers

as they grow and bloom and finally brown
in a pointillist landscape. I have stood under you,

in rain. And I've seen your nests, dark masses
against the sky. You rattle, slant the light,

and grow. Yet you are still young. You give
evidence—that what is used is not always used up.

But today I stand at your feet wanting you
to tell me something. I can't love you more

than I do—you are too cold, too remote. I think
of the averted eyes of a former love, freshly enthralled

with the world, who has discovered it was never
about me to begin with.

For the Attenuated

> *Praise, my dear one.*
> *Let us disappear into praising.*
> *Nothing belongs to us.*
> —Rilke, from "Elegy for Marina"

I seem attenuated, my friend the physicist
tells me. I think I know what he means. I am

stretched thin by grief, the taut wire of my life
grown weak. I wear it on my face, show it

in my crawl through the day, nights populated
with dreams of the missing. He says it

as though he fears me. But I am not a graven
image, a token of anguish to be looked on.

We are all living in extremis, attached, tensile,
to this wire. Swifts caught in the air above

the tipu trees, starlings wound around a belfry
as on a guide rope. We are all in thrall

to the earth—a line of seagulls, lit by the sunset,
forming a ladder to the sea. We are held

together by what has sliced us open. The tide
comes to shore and rushes back out to meet

itself. Here is your grief, on my face. My
gaping heart knowing yours.

Each Spring, These Words

It is my habit to walk the main road
into the marsh, after lifting and letting down

the heavy latch at the gate. I don't have a name
for this road of fine dust and ants, nor does the road

have a name for itself. It just leads to smaller roads,
to paths, and then to trails photographers make

as the waters ebb and flow—the narrowest of all,
and most temporary. These in turn lead to watery

nooks, low branches creating green rooms
of shattered light for mallards and egrets, the priestly

heron. I have a name for the hot road that leads
to a bend in the fence: Kansas Road, for the tall

bush-sunflowers that bound it every spring. And the far
road, under sycamore, I call Ripe Apple Lane

for its scent when the leaves are down and dying.
It is my habit to make my way to the water, follow

the barking geese, the wailing loon. Once, here
at this bridge, I startled a cormorant, dark as the shadow

it hulked in. It rose suddenly, completely. When birds
charge me I know enough to go. They flock and flit

in some small grove, busy with speech, and send guards
to fly at my knees, the back of my head. The goose's eyes

follow me, neck bent, as I back away. It is my habit
to take a notebook, to take every path I come to, though

it often means retracing my steps. It is my habit to feel
alone there, wanting and not wanting someone else

close by. I liked best the time my love waited quietly
behind me as I traced the language of seeds and twigs,

blossoms from the trees, on the passing water. Their shapes
and reflections. We couldn't speak. I could not see him.

I have never understood the script on the water, only
that it moves like a slow river. And inscriptions in the form

of the fallen continue to fall, are etched into the trembling
water, flow past. Each spring, these words.

Brother

My first other
There when my world began

You were no god to me
cruel babysitter

allotter of M&Ms
forced channel changing

and early sendings to bed
You were rogue discipline

shooter of beer cans
wielder of knife

quick hum and grin
but quiet protector

You learned the heart
can erupt without presentiment

vowed to go forward
in wisdom and with care

You became lord
of the lawn, of blue

and placid waters
Oh my Ancient of Days

young as a father
as a son

you are all ages to me
elemental, like breath

like home
You were there

from the beginning
and shall be unto the end

and when I am farthest
from home, alone

in a strange city, I wake
and invoke your name

It comes to me
unbidden

Among the Ruins

Something was already the matter
    with me. I loved the ruin of the house
        even as a child. The broken garden wall,
            the half-fallen crabapple tree, the uneven

sidewalks. I'd walk the steps up and down
    alongside the narrow house that descended
        the hill, around the mountain laurel, past
            the heavy heart-shaped rock—not thinking

about the painful day we brought it home—
    to the landing at the kitchen, then down
        to the yard, which also descended the hill.
        I thought the world was hills then, always

one at my back, protector. Or my way forward. Again
    and again I'd walk from the upper sidewalk
        to the cellar door, approving of each bit
            of moss, each sidewalk crack, the way green

was taking over, steadily, silently. Ignoring the memory
    of the ice sheets the steps became when the salt box
        was empty, and putting aside all memories of anyone
            crying here, I'd imagine standing on this spot

a thousand years earlier, before my family
    sprung up on this land, before coal mines
        gutted the hills, before those dark bores
            began to subside, taking the houses

and sidewalks with them. What kind of fugitive creature
    was I, living outside of time, preparing
        for my eventual exile? Even then I was more
            observer than inhabitant. I loved the ruin

like I love a stubblefield, used and let go. Beginning to return
    to what it was, to turn to what it will be. From the yard
        I'd turn around and go back up, to the porch,
            and imagine we never took brushes

from the workbench, filled a Maxwell House can
    with water, and painted the concrete railing
        a deeper shade of itself, each minuscule pebble
            emerging like a fossil.

Summer Nights, I Fall Asleep on the Back Porch

and wake to a yard that has tasted
its wild roots. Overnight the grass

has grown beyond its measured height,
impatiens ready to burst, the spruce unkempt,

bearing shrouds of fog in its arms.
The groundhog has undermined the earth

once again. The dampness that covers
my blanket, the grass, has got at the essence

and replenished it. So much is held
in those moments before daybreak,

in that dark prescience. The birds know—
they call to it and I listen. I don't have

to ascend or descend or cross some dark
river. I just have to step off the porch,

some evocative morning, into the lost
world of the yard, the risen girl, something

rising in me, something ragged, wild
and wanting.

That Autumn in Pennsylvania

Little has given me so much joy
as to walk quietly into that field of horses

early each Saturday, the smell of earth and animal
sweet and musky, to look for the reddish

freckled one called Strawberry. To approach her
as I would a loved one sleeping. I'd let her

notice me, run my hand along the length
of her neck, speak low and sing-song

of the morning's innocence. Of her warmth.
I could be tethered to this earth forever, forgetting

what our bodies lose every moment to the open
air. Our exhalations rising in clouds, disappearing

into the fields of the sky. Here is the scent
and warmth of uneven ground. And breath enough

for large and small breathing bodies. Taking
her reins I start walking. Her ponderous hooves

lift and follow. When her head swings down
for a scratch across my wool sweater,

I feel the weight of her. Such large love
so late in the year.

To the Animal

To the cat, which comes running
at the opening of a tuna can: you

are fed and watered like the plants
and given more affection.

You open your soft belly to me, hold
no higher pursuits. You will not

take from me.
To the animal Disease, and to your

more feral brother Disillusion:
you are a lion pack circling

the night, pitiless. Make
the night short.

To the animal I've become, with
all my mean desires, for mere

life and ordinary days, all
greed and licking the plate, arms

encircling what is mine: rise
above it when you can.

To the animal biding its time,
that hibernates till half its winter

weight is gone, emerging ravenous:
make of me a quick meal.

And to the hawk, tearing apart
a mourning dove outside my window:

thank you for the sight of a wingbone
pirouetting through leaf-light. You

teach me to open my mouth, release
what is not needed, to the air

or to gravity, whichever will take it.

Between Waves

I dig and find mussel shells
flayed   midnight blue paint

peeling   and bean clams
clackety little pistachio

half-shells with sleek
purple bellies   Sometimes

an arc of color
comes across   a tiny

saddle-shoe   But there is a lip
of land where my real treasures

lie   and the waves
hit that lip   hard

In the great silences between
I run   choose quickly

collect what the sea has worked
brackets   hinges

great connectors half an inch
thick   hardware

that still holds   though
what it held is lost   I covet

these ruins   the curve
of an amphitheater wall

the pleated skirt
of an alabaster woman

thick as marble   thin
as fingernails

the open   not meant
to be open

pink hollow of a mollusk
whorl and fold   like the inner

ear   that delicate column
I rescue them as the sea

in its eternal forgetting
re-forms itself   over and over

in the great lathe
of our unmaking

Grief Is Thorns on the Orange Tree

Heavy flowerhead
        heavy fruit

Grief
        is a magnolia petal

a helpless hand, open
        a starched tablecloth

for the bee
        Or the extant wing

of a moth, breathless
        as heat

An uprooted tree
        with skirts

of unpacked earth
        what stirs, what emerges

from that open grave
        what reburies

itself
        Grief is the sweetgum

most heartbreaking
        in autumn

It is the cattail
        suede coat open

its feathery breast
        ready for the wind

And it is the wind
        its unknowable sowing

Bread = Snow

Know that you will wake
            to snow
     white   crust   pillow

Measure the forecast
            in loaves   the silver ratio

The path   the storm
                 an unsworn oath   How it will
    unfold   lies somewhere
           between bread & snow
    Who knows
            how much the shaggy   milk-goat sky   will give

But below
      the line   of perpetual snow
          prepare   for the sift
   & drift   of coming quiet   Buy bread
    white-flour & water   What is owned

  What is   enough   Nothing
    gets through   What's left
          scatter   for the winter bird
  Bread on the snow

The world a flock
        of silent sheep
               & everything you know
   below

Openings

Trypophobia—the fear of repeated, clustered openings. What may lurk, what may crawl

out. Like the spongy back of the sea toad, which holds its young, who emerge with sticky hands. Or wounds.

Or lotus seeds. In those affected, the mere sight brings on tingling, a burning neck, hard breathing.

I think about other openings—windows, doors. The openings of the face, the small cluster of the eyes. What depths,

what darknesses lie there. The tiny spaces between stitches in wool or cotton, the complexities we bear

on our backs. The watered earth, permeable. Holes birds bore in cactus, in bark. Printed words, aperture after aperture,

enclosed as in *o* and *d*. Or open: *c* and *u* bleeding their emptiness onto the page. I think of the open strands of galaxies,

repeating. Honeycombs, cells, vents. A chain-link fence. Whatever strains, sifts, screens. Whatever excludes. The distances

between seasons, arrayed along the year. The distance between him and me, and the other hims, arrayed along my life. The spaces

between contentment and wondering, between my fear of leaving and the bravery it took to go. The wide spaces that had opened

between us, that I could not fuse alone. The gap between the door and the frame, where I could glimpse him in the other room.

The distance I finally refused to go. Solidity has its own faults—
his hard chest, his hard name. But there are the clusters of hours

in which I am alone. The puncture wounds where love leaches out.
The possible holes in my future. Though I fear these spaces,

they have allowed in light, like overlapping shade, leaf
to leaf. They are the vessels into which I pour my self,

this mouth of regular feedings, these bones, though porous,
still stitched. Strong marrow. Allowing a fluidity

of movement, from happiness to possible happiness.

Dead as I Am

Dead as I am
        in your life
I haunt you

        emerge as
from some
        dream and

I am there
        fetal, in a
corner

        hearing you, your low
mutter, the click
        of your shoelace tips

I open
        my eyes so
I can tell myself:

        the last time
I saw you, you
        were dressing

and looked
        a little tired
Dead as

        I am I come alive
then
        in that room

of you, wake
 to you
breathe

 as quietly
as three a.m.
 My breath

becomes the furnace
 hum
becomes your

 sigh
becomes all
 your soft sounds

becomes the air
 within
the shirt

 you hold
I leave the sleeve
 as you slide

it on and
 when you
go I go

Overcast

> *More dim than waning moon*
> *Thy face, more faint*
> *Than is the falling wind*
> *Thy voice...*
>   *—from "Old Love," by Adelaide Crapsey*

It is springtime in the shadowlands
where no sun-washed dreams of paradise

dwell. Clouds, dove-gray and low, sit soft
above the blooming jacaranda, bluer

than a blue sky. The mourning dove's cry
falls in couplets from the tree, and blossoms

swoon lighter than air around my feet.
I don't need to know the color of the sky

above the cloud bank or how deep this earth
goes. But I need this small cosmos

between cloud cover and garden bed. They say
if you hear the mourning dove's call

and there is no answer, the call was meant for you
in remembrance of a love you've lost. I sing

the mourning dove's song of the overcast.
Soft bleat, mild wail. There is no heaven

like that song.

In Advent

When time slows, almost stops, each breath
        an expansive moment of rising

and falling, as a mountain rises and falls,
        each heartbeat an epoch of snowmelt

and glaciation, and then recedence: there is
        a freshening throughout you. You feel it

as a cloak, cold and white as the moon, and as round,
        around your shoulders. You shiver into it

like an icy dive. This is how it feels to let
        go, like the first glide onto a lake, the shower

of ice, the quietening. This is your first scent
        of winter, the slower tempo, the Hunter

in his place among the stars. You must let yourself
        down into it, open your mouth to the frigid

air, let it arrest you, and begin to breathe
        as the moon breathes. What you can accomplish

there: words written in a needle's eye, poems
        on a fishhook, curved to the metal. Sculpture

in the space of half a breath. This is not falling
        asleep. Though it can be. It can be allowed to be.

Beverly **Voigt** is a winner of the Friends of Acadia Poetry Prize (judged by Wesley McNair) and a Pushcart Prize nominee. Her chapbook *Woman of Salt* was published by Seven Kitchens Press as part of its 2018 Summer Kitchen series. Her poems have appeared in journals such as *Crab Creek Review* and *Sonora Review*. Born and raised in Pittsburgh, Pennsylvania, she currently lives in the South Bay area of Los Angeles and works as an editor and layout specialist.

www.ingramcontent.com/pod-product-compliance
Lightning Source LLC
LaVergne TN
LVHW041603070426
835507LV00011B/1291